Food and Festivals

A Flavour of Kenya

Wambui Kairi

HODDER
Wayland

an imprint of Hodder Children's Books

Other titles:

Cover photograph: A fruit seller with a basket of ripe bananas.

Title page: A Samburu mother with her newborn baby.

Contents page: A woman preparing *ugali*, a dish made from corn flour.

All Wayland books encourage children to read and help them improve their literacy.

✓ The contents page, page numbers, headings and index help locate specific pieces of information.

✓ The glossary reinforces alphabetic knowledge and extends vocabulary.

✓ The further information section suggests other books dealing with the same subject.

✓ Find out more about how this book is specifically relevant to the National Literacy Strategy on page 31.

First published in Great Britain in 1999 by Wayland Publishers Limited

First published in paperback in 2002 by Hodder Wayland, an imprint of Hodder Children's Books

© Hodder Wayland 1999

Hodder Children's Books
A division of Hodder Headline Limited
338 Euston Road, London NW1 3BH

Series editor: Polly Goodman
Book editor: Alison Cooper
Designer: Tim Mayer
Picture researcher: Shelley Noronha

British Library Cataloguing in Publication Data
Kairi, Wambui
A Flavour of Kenya. – (Food and festivals)
1. Cookery, Kenyan – Juvenile literature
2. Festivals – Kenya – Juvenile literature
3. Food habits – Kenya – Juvenile literature
4. Kenya – Social life and customs – Juvenile literature
I. Title
641.5'96762

ISBN 0 7502 4249 3

Typeset by Mayer Media
Printed and bound in Hong Kong

CONTENTS

Kenya and Its Food

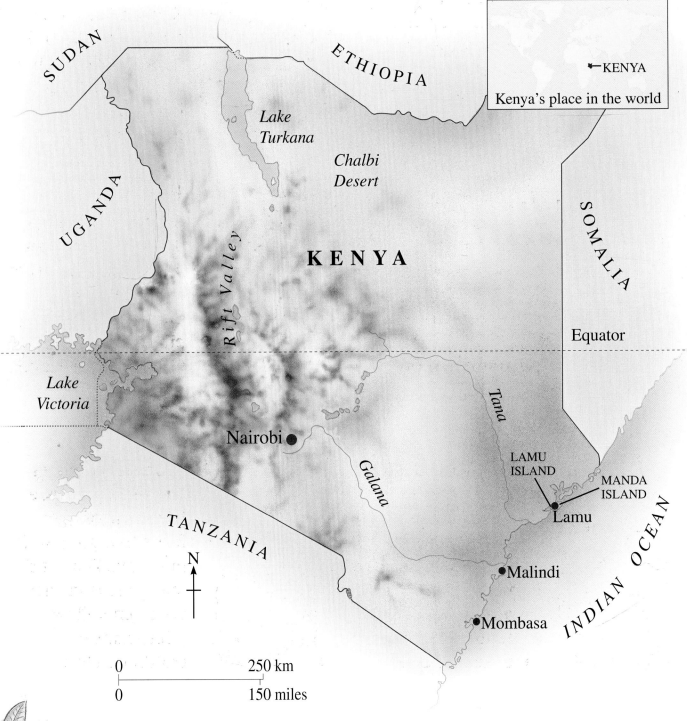

SUDAN

ETHIOPIA

Lake
Turkana

Chalbi
Desert

KENYA

Kenya's place in the world

←KENYA

UGANDA

SOMALIA

Rift Valley

Equator

Lake
Victoria

Tana

Nairobi

Galana

LAMU
ISLAND

MANDA
ISLAND

Lamu

TANZANIA

N

Malindi

Mombasa

INDIAN OCEAN

| 0 | 250 km |
| 0 | 150 miles |

CATTLE, GOATS AND SHEEP

These animals provide meat and milk. In the cities, there is always a scramble to buy live goats to slaughter for the Christmas and New Year feasts.

NUTS

Peanuts and cashew nuts are important ingredients in Kenyan food. Peanuts grow underground. They can be roasted, or made into a paste for sauces or peanut butter.

VEGETABLES

Leafy, green kale is a cheap and very popular vegetable. Kale, carrots and other vegetables are a colourful sight piled up high on market stalls.

TEA

Everyone in Kenya drinks tea, and lots of tea is sold to other countries, too. Thousands of tea pickers are needed to harvest the leaves.

GRAINS AND SEEDS

Flour made from corn can be used to make *ugali,* and millet is used for porridge. *Simsim* (sesame seeds) is sometimes used to make biscuits.

FRUITS

Bananas, mangoes and pineapples are just some of many fruits that grow well in Kenya. During the mango season there are often yellow juice stains on children's clothes!

Food and Farming

Kenya is a tropical country in eastern Africa. It has a coastline on the Indian Ocean and the Equator runs almost through the middle of the country. The climate in Kenya varies from place to place.

Northern and north-eastern Kenya is very hot and dry, and so are parts of the Rift Valley. The peoples who live here include the Maasai, Somali and Samburu. They keep camels, goats and cattle. They move from place to place, looking for fresh pasture and water for their animals.

▼ Kenyan herders with their camels.

Along the coast, the climate is hot and wet. It is hot around Lake Victoria, too, but less humid. Tropical fruits such as mangoes, pawpaws and pineapples grow well in these areas.

If you took a train from the city of Mombasa, on the coast, to the capital, Nairobi, you would really notice the difference in the temperature. Nairobi is on the edge of the cool, wet highlands. Most of Kenya's crops are produced in this area. The climate is especially good for growing tea and coffee.

▲ Traders selling peanuts and cashew nuts. Cashew nuts are picked from trees that grow only along the coast.

▼ A tea picker at work. Only two leaves and a bud are taken from each stem of the bushes, so the tea cannot be harvested by machine.

Staple foods

Vegetables and grains are the traditional staple foods in Kenya. Kale, which is called *sukumawiki* (you say sue-coo-ma-wickie), is eaten with many meals. It is cheap and full of vitamins. Potatoes are becoming a staple food too, especially in the towns and cities. Chips served with chicken and fish provide a cheap lunch for city workers and students.

SUKUMAWIKI, MY LOVE

Kale, or *sukumawiki,* is so popular that there is a poem in its honour:

'All this I am saying
To you all listeners
Is in praise of *sukumawiki*, my love.
Whenever I am hungry, ready is *sukumawiki*.
Sukumawiki, my love, may the Lord bless you.'

(Translated from the Kiswahili poem *'Sukumawiki Kipenzi'* written by Ezekiel Tsinalo)

▼ Two women clear the weeds away from the young kale plants in their vegetable garden.

◀ Farmers harvesting rice by hand, near Mombasa.

▼ A woman prepares a large pot of *ugali* (corn cake).

Rice is grown in central and western Kenya and near the coast. It needs warm weather and a lot of water to grow, so the fields have to be flooded when the rice is planted. Millet, cow peas and black beans are grown in central and western Kenya, too. They can be stored for a long time and eaten during the dry season.

Corn is grown in most parts of the country. The grains can be dried and ground up to produce flour. The flour is used to make porridge and *ugali* (corn cake). *Ugali* is eaten with vegetable and meat stew, or fish.

A herder with his goats. Each goat is marked with a symbol to show which family owns it.

Cattle and poultry

Beef and goat are the meats most often eaten in Kenya. For the herders, meat is the most important part of their everyday diet. As well as eating the meat, the herders sometimes drain a little blood from the necks of live goats and cattle and drink it. It is a good way to get nourishment from their animals without having to kill them.

Chicken is a delicacy in western Kenya. It is the custom for each member of the family to eat a different part of the bird. The men eat the thighs, the women eat the breast meat, boys get the head and neck, and girls are given the wings.

▼ A herder carefully shoots an arrow into a bullock's neck to drain off some of its blood.

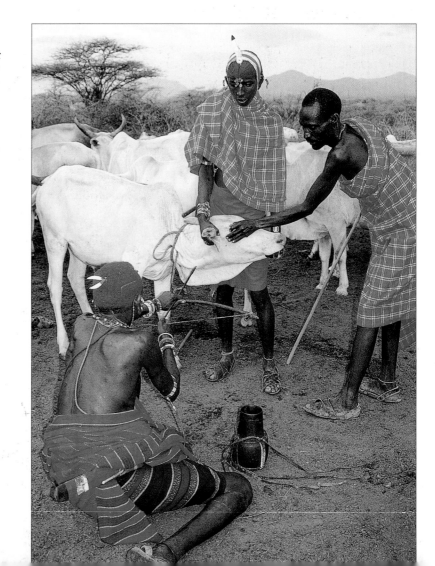

Fish

Fish is an important food for people living along the coast and around the lakes. Most Kenyans love tilapia, a very tasty fish which is a silver-black colour and grows to about 35 cm long. There are many ways of preparing fish. Fried fish is especially popular.

▼ A girl cooks fish, caught in nearby Lake Turkana. She is using palm leaves as fuel, instead of wood.

People and Religions

The people of Kenya are mostly Africans but there are also Asians, Arabs and Europeans. Arab traders were the first non-Africans to arrive in Kenya. Some settled around Mombasa and on Lamu and Manda islands. They brought the Muslim religion to Kenya.

Later, in the fifteenth century, Portuguese explorers arrived. They were Christians. At the end of the nineteenth century the British took control of Kenya, and helped to spread Christianity to more people. They also brought followers of the Hindu religion from India to work for them. In Kenya today, 83 per cent of people are Christians, and there are also many Hindus and Muslims.

▼ A Catholic church service in northern Kenya. The Catholic Church is part of Christianity.

KENYA'S CLANS

African peoples moved into Kenya from other parts of the continent. This is known as the 'great migrations'. The different groups settled in the areas where they live today and formed smaller groups, called clans. For example, the Agikuyu people have nine clans, and one of these is called the Ambui clan.

Some peoples, such as the Maasai, Turkana, Ngiriama and Ameru, follow traditional African religions. They believe in one, all-powerful God, although each of the peoples calls him by a different name, such as Mungu, Allah or Ngai. They believe that the spirits of their ancestors can pass on their thanks and requests for help to God.

▲ This Kikuyu dancer is wearing an elaborate head-dress and face paint because he is taking part in a religious ceremony.

13

Christmas

For Christian children in Kenya, 25 December is the most joyous day of the year. It is Christmas Day, when the birth of Jesus is celebrated. It is also the day when they get new clothes and shoes, and have delicious food to eat. There may be extra gifts for children who have behaved well or done well at school.

CHRISTMAS CARDS

Kenyan Christmas cards used to be imported from Europe. They showed scenes such as Father Christmas in the snow, but most Kenyans had never seen snow. Now there are cards that show Father Christmas riding a camel in the desert. Others show baby Jesus wrapped in a traditional Kenyan cloth called a *kanga*.

◀ This boy's family has decorated the roof of their house with flowers for Christmas.

Christmas brings families together for a big party. The cities are almost deserted because many people prefer to celebrate at their family homes in the country.

Celebrations begin on 24 December, which is Christmas Eve. Young people go from house to house singing Christmas carols. Among the Agikuyu people of central Kenya, this tradition is called *murekio*, which means 'messenger'. The singers are bringing news of the birth of Jesus. They collect gifts too, which they take to church on Christmas Day.

▲ Even this bus in Nairobi has been decorated for Christmas.

Christians practise ▶ Christmas carols.

◀ These children are dressed up for their Nativity play.

At church services on Christmas Eve, people act out the story of Jesus' birth. At their nativity plays they wear traditional African clothes and offer presents such as goats and baskets of grain. They sing African carols and songs to welcome a new baby. There is dancing and music.

▼ These three girls have brought goats to offer to the baby Jesus in a nativity play.

On Christmas day, most Christians go to church. It is mainly women who go to church throughout the year, but on this special day, the men go too. It is hot in Kenya at Christmas time, and after the church service everyone enjoys a chat in the warm sunshine.

Wealthy visitors from the cities bring offerings of money to country churches. Poorer people bring fruit and grain. Their offerings are auctioned to raise money for the work of the church.

▲ These Maasai children have just been to a Christmas Day service in the church behind, where they played their drum.

▲ *Simsim* is the Kenyan word for sesame seeds. *Simsim* biscuits are a Christmas treat in western Kenya. You can find out how to make them on the opposite page.

In the countryside, people go home after church to enjoy a feast. They visit their relatives too, and eat even more food. Everyone enjoys the treats that relatives from the cities bring home with them, such as cakes, fruit juices and bread.

People who stay in the cities at Christmas go out for lunch in a restaurant, or for a picnic. Those who can afford to buy a goat to eat might have a barbecue. People living near the coast sometimes spend the day on the beach.

Simsim Biscuits

INGREDIENTS

150 g Sesame seeds
6 Tablespoons of brown sugar
2 Tablespoons of hot water
A pinch of salt

EQUIPMENT

1 shallow, greased baking tray
Oven gloves
Tablespoon
Mixing bowl

Measuring jug
Kettle
Baking parchment
Palette knife
Round-bladed knife

1 Spread the sesame seeds on a greased baking tray and roast in a preheated oven at 190°C/Gas Mark 6 for about 15 minutes, until they are golden.

2 Boil some water in a kettle. Put the sugar and salt in the bowl and add the hot water. Mix together to make a smooth paste.

3 Stir the sesame seeds into the sugar paste. Spoon the mixture on to a baking tray lined with baking parchment and spread it into a thin layer.

4 Leave the biscuit mixture to harden in the fridge overnight. Then cut it into pieces and eat the biscuits as a snack at any time.

Be careful when using ovens and hot water. Ask an adult to help you.

Ramadan and Id-ul-Fitr

During the month of Ramadan, Muslims fast during the hours of daylight. This means they eat and drink nothing from sunrise until sunset each day. Muslims fast as a way of remembering Allah's goodness to them, for providing them with food.

In the coastal towns of Malindi and Lamu, Muslims own most of the cafés, restaurants and shops. During Ramadan, they usually close them for the whole month, or open only in the evenings to serve *futari*, a light snack to break the fast.

The mosque in ▶ Nairobi, where Muslims go to pray.

Id-ul-Fitr

▲ Muslim women gather to pray at the end of Ramadan.

At the end of Ramadan, there is a day of celebration to break the fast, called Id-ul-Fitr. In Kenya, it is a public holiday. Muslim families exchange gifts and husbands are expected to buy new *kangas* for their wives. Tasty dishes are prepared for a feast. Spiced *pilau* rice is usually served, and people also enjoy *simsim* biscuits, dates and sweets called *halua*.

◄ Delicious snacks are given away to children at the fête.

In Mombasa, a fête is held at the Makadara Muslim Grounds to celebrate Id-ul-Fitr. The fun goes on until late in the evening. The streets are full of people selling different delicacies, from imported dates to cassava chips and bowls of ice-cream and sweets.

Children especially ► like *kaimati*, a small doughnut coated with sugar or grated coconut. You can find out how to make *kaimati* on the opposite page.

22

Kaimati

INGREDIENTS

225 ml Tepid milk

1 Teaspoon of dried yeast

Pinch of sugar

1 Beaten egg

500 g Strong plain flour

1 Teaspoon of salt

Oil for deep frying

Caster sugar or grated coconut

EQUIPMENT

Teaspoon

Measuring jug

Small bowl

Fork

Large bowl

Sieve

Wooden spoon

Clean tea towel

Large pan for deep frying

Tablespoon

Kitchen tongs

Absorbent paper

Large plate

Pour the tepid milk into a small bowl, then sprinkle the dried yeast and a pinch of sugar on the surface. Leave it for about 10 minutes until it looks frothy. Then beat it and stir in the egg.

Sieve the flour and salt into a bowl. Pour in the yeast mixture and stir it in. Form the mixture into a ball of dough and knead it on a floured surface for a few minutes.

Cover the bowl with a damp, clean, tea towel and leave it for 2 hours. Check that the mixture has risen well, and ask an adult to deep-fry spoonfuls of the mixture until golden brown.

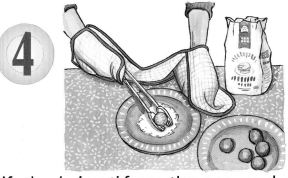

Lift the *kaimati* from the pan, and roll each one in sugar or grated coconut. Leave them to cool on absorbent paper.

Deep-frying can be very dangerous. You must ask an adult to help you.

Naming Ceremonies and Weddings

The birth of a child brings great joy. People come to see the new baby, bringing gifts such as food and baby clothes. Neighbours and relatives help with the cooking and cleaning, so that the new mother can rest.

Among the Kikuyu people of the central province and the Rift Valley, a ceremony called *itega* is held to welcome a new baby. Only women take part in it. They sing songs in praise of the mother and baby. They take turns to hold the baby and spit in each other's foreheads, as a blessing.

◀ A mother with her new baby. She is a member of the Samburu people.

24

NAMES AND THEIR MEANINGS

Wayua
(you say Wa-Yoo-a)
A girl belonging to the Mukamba people, born during the dry, sunny season.

Mutuku
(Moo-TOO-coo)
A Mukamba boy, born during the night.

Njiraini
(N-jer-ARE-nee)
A boy belonging to the Mugikuyu people, born by the roadside.

Wambui
(Wom-BOO-ee)
A Mugikuyu girl belonging to the Ambui clan.

In some Kenyan communities a ceremony is held to give the child a name. Names usually have a meaning that shows the time of day or the season when the child was born, or the place where he or she was born. Some names show who the child's ancestors were.

In country areas, ▶ people often bring firewood as a gift for a new mother.

Weddings

The Agikuyu people have a traditional wedding ceremony called *ngurario*. During the ceremony the bride is hidden by her girlfriends. Sometimes she disguises herself. The groom spends a lot of time looking for her, with the help of his friends. If he does not find her, then he does not marry her.

The bride and groom serve a special wine called *muratina* to the elders. A ram is slaughtered and specific parts are given to men and women. The young girls are given the ram's ears, to remind them to listen to their husbands! Instead of cutting a cake, the groom cuts the roasted leg of a ram.

A delicious tropical fruit punch ▶ is a treat for special celebrations. Find out how to make it on the opposite page.

▲ A bride, bridegroom, bridesmaid and best man (from right to left) bless the herd of goats they have been given as a wedding present.

26

Tropical Fruit Punch

EQUIPMENT

Chopping board   Tablespoon

Sharp knife   Measuring jug

Large jug or fruit bowl

INGREDIENTS (for 6)

2 Bananas

100 g Strawberries, washed

1 Pawpaw, peeled

2 Tablespoons of brown sugar

100 ml Orange juice

100 ml Pineapple juice

100 ml Mango juice

750 ml soda water

12 Ice cubes

1 Slice the bananas into rings and the strawberries into halves. Put them in the jug or fruit bowl.

2 Chop the pawpaw into small cubes and put them in the jug or bowl. Add the brown sugar and stir it in gently.

3 Pour in the fruit juices.

4 Pour in the soda water and stir the mixture gently. Add the ice cubes and serve in tall glasses.

Be careful using knives. Ask an adult to help you.

Thanksgiving

Many Kenyans take part in thanksgiving celebrations. During Mass on New Year's Eve, Catholics give thanks for all the good things they have received in the past year. In September, Anglicans give thanks for the harvest. They take gifts of food to church.

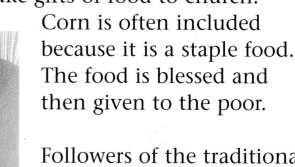

Corn is often included because it is a staple food. The food is blessed and then given to the poor.

Followers of the traditional African religions give thanks to God whenever there is a good harvest and plenty of rain for their animals. During the thanksgiving ceremony, a ram or bull is sacrificed. Some meat is left under a tree as an offering to God.

◄ There is a recipe for this spicy corn dish on the opposite page.

Spicy Corn

INGREDIENTS (for 2)

2 Corn-cobs, washed

1/2 Teaspoon of chilli powder

1/2 Teaspoon of salt

1 Large lemon

EQUIPMENT

Large saucepan

Kitchen tongs

Teaspoon

Small bowl

Sharp knife

Chopping board

Oven gloves

Plate

1 Put the corn cobs into a saucepan of boiling water. Make sure the water covers the cobs. Boil them until they are tender.

2 Mix the chilli powder with the salt in a small bowl. Cut the lemon into two round halves and remove the seeds.

3 Pour the chilli/salt mixture on to the lemon halves. Squeeze the lemon so that the juice soaks the chilli mixture.

4 Carefully take the cobs out of the pan and put them on a large plate. Rub a lemon half over each cob and eat them hot.

Be careful when using knives and hot pans. Ask an adult to help you.

Glossary

Allah The Muslim name for God.

Ancestors Family members who lived, and died, a long time ago.

Anglicans Christians who worship in a similar way to people in the Church of England.

Auctioned Sold to the person who offers the highest price (instead of being sold for a fixed price, like goods in a supermarket).

Catholics Christians who are led by the Pope in Rome, Italy.

Climate The type of weather that an area usually has.

Equator The imaginary line that runs around the centre of the Earth, half-way between the North and South Poles.

Humid The weather is humid when it is warm and there is a lot of moisture in the air, although it is not actually raining.

Imported Brought in from another country.

Kanga A large cloth with traditional patterns printed on it, which can be worn like a dress.

Mass An important religious ceremony celebrated by Catholics.

Migration The movement of large numbers of people (or animals) from one place to another.

Muslims People who follow the religion called Islam.

Sacrificed Killed as an offering to God, as part of a religious ceremony.

Staple foods Foods that people eat with most everyday meals.

Tropical Between the Tropics of Cancer and Capricorn on the world map. Tropical areas have hot, wet weather all year round.

Ugali A savoury dish made from corn flour, usually eaten with stews.

Picture acknowledgements

Steve Benbow 7; Chris Brown Educational 15 (bottom); Chapel Studios/Zul Mukhida 5 (bottom left), 18,22 (bottom), 26 (bottom), 28; Robert Harding 5 (top left)/Thomasin Magor, 6/N.A. Callow, 10 (top)/Thomasin Magor; Images of Africa *cover*/Carla Signorini Jones, *title page*, 5 (top right and bottom right)/Carla Signorini Jones, 10 (bottom)/Carla Signorini Jones, 12/David Keith Jones, 16 (lower)/David Keith Jones, 24/Carla Signorini Jones, 25/David Keith Jones, 26 (top)/David Keith Jones; Impact 9 (top)/Caroline Penn; Peter Kenward *contents page*, 5 (centre right), 7 (bottom), 9 (bottom), 22 (top); Oxfam (G.Sayer) 17; Panos 5 (centre left)/ Betty Press, 8/Betty Press, 11/Lana Wong, 21/Betty Press; Ann & Bury Peerless 16 (top); Tony Stone Images 13/Art Wolfe; Tropix 14/J.Schmid, 15/J.Schmid; Zefa-Stockmarket 20/M.M Lawrence. Fruit and vegetable artwork by Tina Barber. Map artwork on page 4 by Hardlines. Step-by-step recipe artwork by Judy Stevens.

Topic Web and Resources

MATHS

Use and understand data and measures (recipes).

Use and understand fractions.

Use and read measuring instruments: scales.

SCIENCE

Food and nutrition.

Separating mixtures of materials: sieving.

Changing materials through heat.

Plants in different habitats.

GEOGRAPHY

Locality study.

Weather

Farming and how land is used.

Comparing physical landscapes.

Influences of landscape on human activities: where they live, farming and food festivals.

HISTORY

Traditions of different Kenyan peoples.

Colonialism

Food & Festivals TOPIC WEB

MUSIC

Find out about traditional instruments used at festivals.

R.E.

Christian festivals.

Muslim festivals.

Traditional African religions.

DESIGN AND TECHNOLOGY

Look at traditional patterns and design a *kanga*.

ENGLISH

Make up a slogan to sell a popular Kenyan food, such as *ugali*.

BOOKS TO READ

Country Insights: Kenya by Máiréad Dunne, Wambui Kairi and Eric Nyaanjom (Wayland, 1997)

We Come From Kenya by Wambui Kairi (Wayland, 1999)

World Focus: Kenya by David Marshall & Geoff Sayer (Heinemann, 1994)

PHOTO AND EDUCATIONAL PACKS

Kapsakwony: a village in Kenya A case study of a family in a village in Western Kenya (ActionAid, 1992)

Nairobi: Kenya City Life A case study of a poor community in the slum area of Kariobangi, Nairobi (ActionAid, 1992)

Feeling Good about Far Away Friends A case study of a Maasai family in Kenya (Leeds DEC, 1995)

USEFUL ADDRESSES

Kenya High Commission, 45 Portland Place, London W1N 4AS (Tel:0207 636 2371)

This book meets the following specific objectives of the National Literacy Strategy's Framework for Teaching:

✓ Range of work in non-fiction: simple recipes (especially Year 2, Term 1), instructions, labels, captions, lists, glossary, index.

✓ Vocabulary extension: words linked to particular topics (food words) and technical words from work in other subjects (geography and food science).

Index

Page numbers in **bold** mean there is a photograph on the page.